Chefs' Special

Tikkas & Kebabs

D1343137

Tikkas & Kebabs

*Compiled by
Master Chefs
of India*

Silverdale Books

GOURMET DELIGHT

In a land so rich in cultural heritage, it is but natural that the Indian cuisine is multifarious, offering a delight to both the eye and the palate. Its myriad flavours and cooking traditions find their roots in its historical influences. The Mughals revolutionised the art of Indian cooking with their delectable *biryanis* (an exquisite oven preparation with meat/vegetables, herbs and seasonings), *kormas* (a spicy meat or vegetarian preparation), *kebabs* and *tikkas* (meat and vegetables cooked in small pieces, usually on skewers) made in a *tandoor* (an oven made of mud and heated by a slow charcoal fire). The British Raj spawned an interesting Anglo-Indian gastronomic culture which is still eaten with relish. Different regions in India offer their own specialities with their very own taste, subtlety and aroma. The country's vast reservoir of spices made from its abundance of tropical herbs, serves as garnishing and contains medicinal and preservative properties. Indeed the range of the Indian cuisine can amaze even a connoisseur.

This book brings you a feast of sizzling *Tikkas & Kebabs*. These delectables which include cutlets and chops, can be served as snacks, starters or the main course itself. A few basic recipes of popular cooking ingredients, including *masalas,* Indian equivalents of foods given in each list of Ingredients and a Glossary of Cooking Terms are valuable add-ons. A multi-purpose chutney, pickle and relishing *rotis* (pp. 88-91) serve as a complimentary fillip. And to provide a finishing touch, a sprinkling of 'handy hints' are added as sure-fire remedies to common culinary problems.

BASIC INDIAN RECIPES

Green Chilli Paste
Chop the required quantity of green chillies and process until pulped.

Garam Masala (for 450 gm)
Put 200 gm cumin, 35 gm peppercorns, 45 gm black cardamoms, 30 gm green cardamoms, 60 gm coriander seeds, 20 gm cloves, 20 gm cinnamon sticks, 15 gm bayleaves and 2 nutmegs in a processor and grind to a fine powder. Transfer to a bowl, add 20 gm mace powder and 30 gm ginger powder and mix well. Sieve and store in an airtight container.

Brown Onion Paste
Fry sliced onions over medium heat till brown. Drain excess oil and allow to cool. Process until pulped, (using very little water, if required). Refrigerate in an airtight container.

Yoghurt
Boil milk and keep aside till lukewarm. Add 2 tsp yoghurt to the milk and mix well. Allow to ferment for 6-8 hours.

Red Chilli Paste
Chop red chillies and process until pulped.

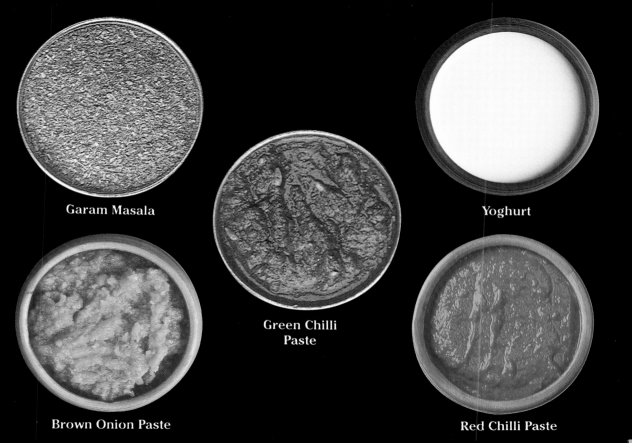

Garam Masala

Green Chilli
Paste

Yoghurt

Brown Onion Paste

Red Chilli Paste

Ginger/Garlic Paste
Soak ginger/garlic overnight. Peel, chop and process to pulp. Refrigerate in an airtight container.

Onion Paste
Peel and quarter onions and process until pulped. Refrigerate in an airtight container.

Tomato Purée
Peel, deseed and chop the tomatoes. Transfer to a pan, add 1 lt water, 8 cloves, 8 green cardamoms, 15 gm ginger, 10 gm garlic, 5 bayleaves and 5 peppercorns and cook on medium heat till the tomatoes are tender. Cool and process to a pulp.

Cottage Cheese (*Paneer*)
Heat 3 lt milk. Just before it boils, add 60 ml/4 tsp lemon juice or white vinegar. Strain the milk through a muslin cloth and hang for 2-3 hours to drain the whey and moisture.

Khoya
Boil milk in a wok (*kadhai*). Reduce heat and cook, stirring occasionally, till the quantity is reduced to half. Then stir constantly and scrape from all sides till a thick paste-like consistency is obtained. Allow to cool. *Khoya* is also called wholemilk fudge.

Ginger-Garlic Paste

Cottage Cheese

Onion Paste

Tomato Purée

Khoya

BADAM KE SHAMMI KEBAB

(Minced lamb kebabs flavoured with almonds)

Serves: 4   Preparation time: 1 hour   Cooking time: 20 minutes

Ingredients

Lamb, minced *1 kg*
Bengal gram (*chana dal*) *30 gm / 2 tsp*
Red chillies, whole *5*
Green chillies, whole *5*
Black cardamoms (*bari elaichi*) *5*
Bayleaves (*tej patta*) *5*
Cinnamon (*dalchini*) sticks *5*
Cloves (*laung*) *10*
Water *2 lt / 10 cups*
Eggs *3*
Salt *10 gm / 2 tsp*
Almonds (*badam*), slivered
60 gm / ¼ cup
Oil for frying

Method

1. Boil the mince with Bengal gram, red chillies, green chillies and all the whole spices in water till the water evaporates.

2. Remove the whole spices from the mince and discard. Mash the mince well.

3. Add eggs and salt to the mixture and knead it well. Sprinkle almonds and mix well.

4. Divide the mixture into even-sized balls and shape into cutlets.

5. Heat oil in a wok *(kadhai)* and deep fry the cutlets until crisp and brown on all sides.

6. Remove, drain excess oil and serve hot.

BOTI KEBABS

(Succulent pieces of lamb barbecued to perfection)

Serves: 4   Preparation time: 2 hours 30 minutes   Cooking time: 20-25 minutes

Ingredients

Lamb, cut into boneless pieces *1 kg*
Ginger-garlic *(adrak-lasan)* paste
(p. 8) *90 gm / ½ cup*
Salt to taste
Lemon juice *75 ml / 5 tbsp*
Raw papaya *(kacha papita)* paste
60 gm / ¼ cup
Yoghurt *(dahi)* (p. 6), hung
60 gm / ¼ cup
White pepper *(safed mirch)* powder
5 gm / 1 tsp
Cumin *(jeera)* powder *5 gm / 1 tsp*
Green cardamom *(choti elaichi)*
powder *5 gm / 1 tsp*
Red chilli powder *10 gm / 2 tsp*

Oil *100 ml / ½ cup*
Butter for basting

Method

1. Wash and clean the lamb pieces. Marinate them with ginger-garlic paste, salt, lemon juice and raw papaya paste. Keep aside for 30 minutes.
2. Prepare a second marinade by mixing all the other ingredients. Marinate the lamb cubes with this marinade and keep aside for 2 hours.
3. Skewer the lamb cubes and roast in a tandoor/oven/grill for 15-20 minutes. Remove, baste with butter and roast again for 3-5 minutes.
4. Remove from skewers and serve hot.

COCKTAIL KEBABS

Serves: 4-6   Preparation time: 1 hour 30 minutes   Cooking time: 30 minutes

Ingredients

Lamb, minced ½ kg
Bengal gram *(chana dal)*, split
115 gm / ½ cup
Red chillies, dried, chopped 4-5
Onions (medium), chopped 2
Salt to taste
Ginger *(adrak)*, chopped 10 gm / 2 tsp
Garam masala (p. 6) 8 gm / 1 ½ tsp
Egg, slightly beaten 1
For the filling:
Green coriander *(hara dhaniya)*,
chopped 6 gm / 1 tsp
Green chillies, finely chopped
15 gm / 1 tbsp
Onions, finely chopped 60 gm / 4 tbsp
Salt to taste
Oil for frying

Method

1. Boil minced meat along with Bengal gram, red chillies, onions, salt and ginger in 4 cups of water till the meat and gram are tender. Strain the liquid.
2. Grind the mince very finely, add the garam masala and beaten egg and knead well. Divide into 20 equal portions and keep aside.
3. For the filling, mix chopped onions, green chillies, coriander leaves and salt. Divide into 20 equal parts.
4. Flatten each part of the mince, put one part of stuffing in the centre and shape into balls, wetting your hands if necessary.
5. Heat oil in flat pan till it starts smoking. Deep fry the kebabs, a few at a time, till crisp and brown.
6. Serve hot, garnished with onion rings.

POTATO-COATED LAMB CHOPS

Serves: 4-5   Preparation time: 1 hour 30 minutes   Cooking time: 30 minutes

Ingredients

Lamb chops *12*
Water *600 ml / 3 cups*
Onion, (medium) sliced *1*
Ginger *(adrak)*, sliced *5 gm / 1 tsp*
Garlic *(lasan)* cloves *6*
Peppercorns *(kali mirch) 6-8*
Cinnamon *(dalchini)* stick (1") *1*
Black cardamoms *(bari elaichi) 2*
Cloves *(laung) 4*
Salt to taste

For the coating:
Potatoes, boiled, peeled, mashed *½ kg*
Ginger *(adrak)*, finely chopped
5 gm / 1 tsp
Green chillies, finely chopped *2*
Coriander *(dhaniya)*, chopped
15 gm /1 tbsp

Black pepper *(kali mirch)* powder *3 gm / ½ tsp*
Red chilli powder *3 gm / ½ tsp*
Salt to taste
Breadcrumbs, powdered

Method

1. Put the chops in a pan. Add water, sliced onions, ginger, garlic, peppercorns, cinnamon, cardamoms, cloves and salt. Cover the pan and let the chops simmer on low heat till tender. Remove from the stock and keep aside.

2. For the coating, add ginger, green chillies, coriander, black pepper powder, red chilli powder and salt to the potatoes. Mix well.

3. Divide the potato mixture into 12 portions.

4. Moisten palm and spread one portion of the potato mixture on it. Place a chop in the middle and wrap

mashed potato around it, shaping it well. Prepare the remaining chops similarly and keep aside.

5. Spread the powdered breadcrumbs in a flat tray. Coat each chop evenly with the breadcrumbs and keep aside.

6. Heat oil in a wok (*kadhai*) till it starts smoking.

7. Fry the chops, two at a time, till they are crisp and nicely browned from all sides.

8. Drain on a paper napkin and serve with salad.

———— ❖ ————

Party with an Easy-to-Make Pudding

Boil 2 cups milk with 3 tsp sugar. Add small pieces of bread, a little drops of vanilla essence. Mix well and bake for 45 minutes.

———— ❖ ————

MALAI SEEKH KEBABS

(Minced lamb kebabs, with herbs and cashewnuts)

Serves: 4-5   Preparation time: 25 minutes   Cooking time: 15 minutes

Ingredients

Lamb, minced *900 gm / 4 ½ cups*
Cashewnut *(kaju)* paste *75 gm / ⅓ cup*
Eggs, whisked *2*
Garam masala (p. 6) *10 gm / 2 tsp*
Ginger *(adrak)*, finely chopped
40 gm / 2 ⅔ tbsp
Green chillies, finely chopped *8*
Green coriander *(hara dhaniya)*,
finely chopped *20 gm / 4 tsp*
Lamb kidney fat *150 gm / ¾ cup*
Oil *50 ml / 3 ⅓ tbsp*
Onions, finely chopped
40 gm / 2 ⅔ tbsp
Salt to taste
White pepper *(safed mirch)* powder
3 gm / ⅔ tsp
Butter for basting *50 gm / 3 ⅓ tbsp*

Method

1. Add all the ingredients, except butter, to the lamb mince and mix well. Keep aside for 15 minutes.
2. Divide into 12 equal portions and make into balls. Preheat the tandoor / oven to 160 °C / 320 °F. Press the balls with moistened palms along the skewers, 8-10 cm long each and about 4 cm apart. Roast for 8-10 minutes.
3. Remove and hang the skewers to let the excess moisture drip off.
4. Baste with butter and roast again for 2 minutes.
5. Garnish with onion rings, lemon wedges and shredded cabbage or carrots.

FENUGREEK-FLAVOURED, GRILLED LAMB CUBES

Serves: 4-5   Preparation time: 3 hours 30 minutes   Cooking time: 20 minutes

Ingredients

Lamb (leg or shoulder),
cut into boneless cubes *1 kg*
Ginger-garlic *(adrak-lasan)* paste
(p. 8) *90 gm / 6 tbsp*
Vinegar *(sirka) 45 ml / 3 tbsp*
Red chilli powder *10 gm / 2 tsp*
Black pepper *(kali mirch)*, ground
5 gm / 1 tsp
Salt to taste
Cream *45 gm / 3 tbsp*
Cheese *45 gm / 3 tbsp*
Garam masala (p. 6) *5 gm / 1 tsp*
Cumin *(jeera)* powder *5 gm / 1 tsp*
Saffron *(kesar)* a pinch
Dry fenugreek *(kasoori methi)*
powder *3 gm / ½ tsp*
Butter for basting

Method

1. Mix ginger-garlic paste, vinegar, red chilli powder, black pepper and salt together.

2. Marinate the lamb cubes in the prepared mixture for 2 hours.

3. In another bowl, mix cream, cheese, garam masala, cumin powder, saffron and fenugreek powder. Add marinated lamb to this mixture and set aside for 1 hour.

4. Preheat oven to 175 °C / 350 °F. Skewer the lamb cubes, 2 cm apart. Roast in oven/charcoal grill/tandoor for 8-10 minutes. Hang skewers for a few minutes to allow excess liquids to drip. Baste with butter and cook for another 3-4 minutes.

5. Serve hot, garnished with chopped coriander and cream, lemon wedges and onion rings.

LAMB SEEKH KEBABS

Serves: 4-5   Preparation time: 25 minutes   Cooking time: 15 minutes

Ingredients

Lamb, minced *900 gm / 4 ½ cups*
Green coriander *(hara dhaniya)*,
finely chopped *10 gm / 2 tsp*
Green cardamom *(choti elaichi)*
powder *3 gm / ½ tsp*
Cottage cheese *(paneer)* (p. 8),
grated *15 gm / 1 tbsp*
Garam masala (p. 6) *20 gm / 4 tsp*
Ginger *(adrak)* paste (p. 8)
45 gm / 3 tbsp
Green chillies, finely chopped
8 gm / 1½ tsp
Lamb kidney fat *150 gm / ¾ cup*
Mace powder *(javitri) 5 gm / 1 tsp*
Brown onion paste (p. 6)
100 gm / ½ cup
Poppy seed *(khus khus)* paste
100 gm / ½ cup

Salt to taste
Butter to baste *60 gm / 4 tbsp*

Method

1. Combine all the ingredients in a bowl. Mix thoroughly and refrigerate for 15 minutes.
2. Divide into 20 equal portions and roll into balls.
3. Preheat oven to 175 °C / 350 °F.
4. Skewer each ball. With wet hands, spread the balls by pressing each along the length of the skewer 4 cm apart, making each kebab 8-10 cm long.
5. Roast in a hot tandoor/oven/charcoal grill for 8-10 minutes.
6. Remove and hang the skewers to let the excess moisture drip off.
7. Baste with butter and roast for another 2 minutes.
8. Garnish with sliced cucumber, tomato slices and onion rings. Serve hot.

EXOTIC LAMB KEBABS

Serves: 4   Preparation time: 1 hour   Cooking time: 20-25 minutes

Ingredients

Lamb, minced *250 gm / 1¼ cups*
Lamb kidney, finely chopped
125 gm / ¾ cup
Lamb liver, finely chopped
125 gm / ¾ cup
Salt *3 gm / ½ tsp*
Red chilli powder *3 gm / ½ tsp*
Garam masala (p. 6) *5 gm / 1 tsp*
Fenugreek *(methi)* powder *a pinch*
Ginger-garlic *(adrak-lasan)* paste
(p. 8) *15 gm / 3 tsp*
Green coriander *(hara dhaniya),*
chopped *10 gm / 2 tsp*
Green chillies, chopped *5 gm / 1 tsp*
Chicken, minced *500 gm / 2 ½ cups*
Salt *3 gm / ½ tsp*
White pepper *(safed mirch)* powder
3 gm / ½ tsp

Fenugreek *(methi)* powder *a pinch*
Butter for basting *20 gm / 4 tsp*

Method

1. Mix together the lamb mince, kidney, liver, salt, red chilli powder, ½ tsp garam masala, fenugreek powder, 2 tsp ginger-garlic paste, 1 tsp green coriander and green chillies. Keep aside.

2. Skewer the mince-mixture and roast in a charcoal grill for 8-10 minutes. Remove and place the skewers upright to allow excess liquids to drip. Keep aside for 3-5 minutes.

3. Meanwhile, mix chicken mince along with all the other ingredients and coat the lamb kebabs evenly with this mixture. Roast again for 5-6 minutes.

4. Baste with butter, remove from skewers and serve, accompanied by salad.

SEEKH KEBABS GILAFI

(Skewered lamb with capsicum)

Serves: 4   Preparation time: 2 hours 30 minutes   Cooking time: 15 minutes

Ingredients

Lamb, minced *1 kg*
Ginger *(adrak)* paste (p. 8)
45 gm / 3 tbsp
Brown onion paste (p. 6)
240 gm / 1¼ cups
Green chillies, minced *6*
Garam masala (p. 6) *10 gm / 2 tsp*
Red chilli powder *10 gm / 2 tsp*
Salt *10 gm / 2 tsp*
Oil *45 ml / 3 tbsp*
Processed cheese *100 gm / ½ cup*
Onions, finely chopped
100 gm / ½ cup
Capsicums *(Shimla mirch)*, finely
chopped *100 gm / ½ cup*
Butter for basting

Tomatoes, deseeded, finely chopped
100 gm / ½ cup

Method

1. Mix the lamb mince with ginger paste, brown onion paste, green chillies, garam masala, red chilli powder, salt, oil and processed cheese.

2. Mix together onions, capsicums and tomatoes.

3. Squeeze out excess water, if any, from the mince mixture and mix thoroughly. Keep aside for 2 hours.

4. Shape the mince mixture along the length of the skewers and coat with the vegetable mixture.

5. Roast in a tandoor/oven/grill for 10-15 minutes, basting with butter at regular intervals. Remove from skewers and serve hot.

BARBECUED LIVER

Serves: 4-6   Preparation time: 3 hours 30 minutes   Cooking time: 30 minutes

Ingredients

Liver, cut into cubes *250 gm*
Ginger *(adrak)* paste (p. 8)
15 gm / 1 tbsp
Garlic *(lasan)* paste (p. 8) *5 gm / 1 tsp*
Onion paste (p. 8) *5 gm / 1 tsp*
Yoghurt *(dahi)* (p. 6) *30 gm / 2 tbsp*
Red chilli powder *3 gm / ½ tsp*
Garam masala (p. 6) *3 gm / ½ tsp*
Cumin *(jeera)* powder *3 gm / ½ tsp*
Green coriander *(hara dhaniya)*,
chopped *10 gm / 2 tsp*
Turmeric *(haldi)* powder *3 gm / ½ tsp*
Carom *(ajwain)* seeds *3 gm / ½ tsp*
Dry fenugreek *(kasoori methi)*
powder *5 gm / 1 tsp*
Salt to taste
Oil *15 ml / 1 tbsp*
Oil / butter for basting

Method

1. Rub ginger, garlic and onion pastes on the liver cubes and set aside for an hour.

2. Mix the remaining ingredients into the yoghurt and evenly coat the liver cubes. Leave to marinate for at least 2 hours.

3. Preheat oven to 150 °C / 300 °F.

4. Thread the cubes gently onto the skewers. Roast / grill / bake till half done (10 minutes).

5. Drain excess liquids, baste once and roast again for 4-5 minutes till cooked through.

6. Serve at once, accompanied by salad.

TANGY MINT LAMB CHOPS

Serves: 4-5   Preparation time: 4 hours   Cooking time:12-15 minutes

Ingredients

Lamb chops,washed *1 kg*
Cumin *(jeera)* powder *5 gm / 1 tsp*
White pepper *(safed mirch)* powder
15 gm /1 tbsp
Garam masala (p. 6) *10 gm / 2 tsp*
Lemon juice *25 ml / 5 tsp*
Salt to taste
Oil for basting
Cream *60 ml / 4 tbsp*
Yoghurt *(dahi)* (p. 6), drained
150 gm / ¾ cup
Mint *(pudina)* chutney
250 gm / 1¼ cups
Cornflour *(makkai ka atta)*
30 gm / 2 tbsp
Papaya *(papita)* paste *45 gm / 3 tbsp*
Garlic *(lasan)* paste (p. 8)
15 gm /1 tbsp

Ginger *(adrak)* paste (p. 8) *15 gm / 1 tbsp*
Dry fenugreek *(kasoori methi) 5 gm / 1 tsp*

Method

1. Mix cumin powder, white pepper, garam masala, lemon juice and salt. Add the lamb chops and marinate for 1 hour.
2. Mix cream, yoghurt, fresh mint chutney and cornflour. Add remaining ingredients and whisk to a fine paste. Add to the lamb chops and marinate for another 2-3 hours.
3. Skewer lamb chops 2 cm apart and roast in a pre-heated oven at 175 °C / 350 °F for 8-10 minutes. Hang skewers to allow excess marinade to drip off. Baste with oil and roast for another 4-5 minutes.
4. Sprinkle lemon juice; garnish with slices of cucumber, tomato and onion and serve hot.

MASALA LAMB STEAKS

Serves: 4   Preparation time: 10 minutes   Cooking time: 7-10 minutes

Ingredients

Lamb steaks (thick slices) (2" x 2") *8*
Onion, minced *1*
Garlic *(lasan)*, crushed *15 gm / 1 tbsp*
Green chilli paste (p. 6) *15 gm / 1 tbsp*
Poppy seeds *(khus khus)*,
ground *15 gm / 1 tbsp*
Garam masala (p. 6) *15 gm / 1 tbsp*
Salt to taste

Method

1. Mix onion, garlic and green chilli paste with poppy seeds, garam masala and salt.

2. Marinate steaks in this mixture for 2 hours.

3. Roast in a charcoal grill/tandoor till cooked as desired.

4. Serve hot, garnished with onion rings and accompanied by pickled green chillies.

STUFFED CHICKEN STEAKS

Serves: 4-5   Preparation time: 40 minutes   Cooking time: 40 minutes

Ingredients

Chicken necks, outer skin / chicken
breasts, skinned, flattened *5 pieces*
For the filling:
Chicken, minced *900 gm / 4½ cups*
Aniseed *(saunf)* powder *3 gm / ½ tsp*
Cheese, grated *25 gm / 5 tsp*
Black pepper *(kali mirch)* powder
5 gm / 1 tsp
Butter to baste *100 gm / ½ cup*
Cream *20 ml / 4 tsp*
Egg *1*
Garam masala (p. 6) *10 gm / 2 tsp*
Ginger-garlic *(adrak-lasan)* paste
(p. 8) *60 gm /4 tbsp*
Green chilli paste (p. 6) *8 gm / 1½ tsp*
Green coriander *(hara dhaniya)*,
chopped *10 gm / 2 tsp*
Lemon juice *15 ml / 1 tbsp*

Nutmeg *(jaiphal)*, grated *½*
Onions, grated *45 gm / 3 tbsp*, Salt to taste

Method

1. Mix all the ingredients, except chicken pieces, with
the chicken mince and refrigerate for 30 minutes.
2. Divide into 5 portions and make into balls. Stuff
each neck right through with a portion of the mixture
and tie a thread on both ends of the stuffed necks. If
using breasts, place each ball in the centre, wrap,
shape like a haggis (heart, lungs or liver of sheep) and
tie with thread. Heat the oven to 150 °C / 300 °F.
3. Grease the roasting tray; arrange the stuffed necks
or stuffed chicken breasts and dot with a little butter.
Roast for 30-40 minutes, turning constantly and
basting with melted butter, until golden in colour.
4. Remove the threads and serve hot.

CHICKEN TIKKAS

Serves: 3-4   Preparation time: 6 hours 30 minutes   Cooking time: 10 minutes

Ingredients

Chicken breasts, cut into
boneless cubes *4*
Yoghurt *(dahi)* (p. 6) *150 ml / ¾ cup*
Garlic *(lasan)* paste (p. 8) *5 gm / 1 tsp*
Ginger *(adrak)*, finely chopped
8 gm / 1½ tsp
Onion (small), grated *1*
Red chilli powder *8 gm / 1½ tsp*
Coriander *(dhaniya)* powder
15 gm / 1 tbsp
Salt to taste
Butter for basting

Method

1. Combine yoghurt, garlic paste, ginger, onion, chilli powder, coriander and salt together in a bowl and mix well. Add chicken cubes to the marinade and coat evenly. Cover the bowl and refrigerate for at least 6 hours or overnight.
2. Skewer the chicken cubes. Roast in a preheated oven/grill/tandoor, turning cubes occasionally, for 8-10 minutes or until cooked thoroughly, basting at least once.
3. Remove cubes from skewers and place on a warmed serving dish. Garnish with onion rings, tomato slices and coriander leaves. Serve at once.

AFGHANI CHICKEN KEBABS

Serves: 4   Preparation time: 4 hours 30 minutes   Cooking time: 15 minutes

Ingredients

Chicken broilers (750 gm each) *2*
Salt to taste
White pepper *(safed mirch)* powder
10 gm / 2 tsp
Ginger *(adrak)* paste (p. 8)
25 gm / 5 tsp
Garlic *(lasan)* paste (p. 8)
25 gm / 5 tsp
Mace *(javitri)* powder *4 gm / ³/₄ tsp*
mixed with malt vinegar *(sirka)*
60 ml / ¹/₃ cup
Yoghurt *(dahi)* (p. 6), hung
400 gm / 2 cups
Cheese, grated *100 gm / ¹/₂ cup*
Cream *60 gm / 4 tbsp*
Green chillies, chopped *6*
Mace *(javitri)* powder *1 ¹/₂ gm / ¹/₃ tsp*

Green cardamom *(choti elaichi)* powder
2 gm / ¹/₃ tsp
Butter for basting *50 gm / 3 ¹/₃ tbsp*

Method

1. Clean, skin and cut each chicken into 12 pieces.
2. In a large bowl, mix salt, white pepper and ginger and garlic pastes with the malt vinegar-cum-mace powder mixture. Rub the chicken pieces with this mixture. Marinate for 1 hour.
3. In another bowl, mix the yoghurt and grated cheese. Add the cream, chopped green chillies, mace and cardamom powder. Mix thoroughly.
4. Transfer the marinated chicken into the yoghurt mixture. Keep aside for 3 hours.
5. Preheat the oven to 175 °C / 350 °F. Skewer the

chicken pieces 2 cm apart. Keep a tray underneath to collect the excess drippings.
6. Roast in a moderately hot oven or tandoor for 10-12 minutes.
7. Remove and hang the skewers to allow the excess liquid to drip off. Baste the chicken with butter and roast for another 3 minutes.
8. Serve the kebabs on a bed of lettuce with lemon wedges.

———— ❖ ————

Say 'C-H-E-E-SE' !

Cheese remains fresh if it is placed on a dish and covered with a wet cloth, rather than inside a lidded dish. If the cheese gets mouldy at the top, simply cut off that portion and use the rest—nothing will be wrong with it.

———— ❖ ————

GINGER CHICKEN KEBABS

Serves: 4   Preparation time: 1 hour 30 minutes   Cooking time: 15 minutes

Ingredients

Chicken breasts, cut into
boneless cubes *1kg*
Green chilli paste (p. 6) *15 gm / 1 tbsp*
White pepper *(safed mirch)*
powder *10 gm / 2 tsp*
Salt to taste
Ginger *(adrak)* paste (p. 8)
60 gm / 4 tbsp
Malt vinegar *20 ml / 4 tsp*
Yoghurt *(dahi)* (p. 6), drained
200 gm / 1 cup
Cream *60 ml / 4 tbsp*
Butter for basting
Ginger *(adrak)*, julienned (long,
thin strips) *10 gm / 2 tsp*

Method

1. Clean the chicken cubes. Mix green chilli paste, white pepper powder, salt, ginger paste and vinegar in a large bowl and rub on the chicken cubes. Keep aside for 30 minutes.

2. Mix yoghurt with cream in a separate bowl. Add the chicken cubes to the mixture and keep aside for half an hour.

3. Skewer chicken cubes and roast in a preheated (175 °C / 350 °F) oven/tandoor/grill for 5-8 minutes. Hang skewers to allow excess liquids to drip. Roast again for 4-5 minutes. Remove from skewers.

4. Serve hot, garnished with julienned ginger.

CHICKEN KEBABS

Serves: 4   Preparation time: 45 minutes   Cooking time: 20 minutes

Ingredients

Chicken, cut into boneless
cubes *900 gm / 4 ½ cups*
Salt *10 gm / 2 tsp*
Dry fenugreek *(kasoori methi)*
powder *3 gm / ½ tsp*
Ginger-garlic *(adrak-lasan)* paste
(p. 8) *30 gm / 2 tbsp*
Green chillies, chopped *10 gm / 2 tsp*
Green coriander *(hara dhaniya)*,
chopped *10 gm / 2 tsp*
Vinegar *(sirka) 5 ml / 1 tsp*
Oil *75 ml / 5 tbsp*
Gram flour *(besan)*, seived
25 gm / 5 tsp
Breadcrumbs, fresh *45 gm / 3 tbsp*
Eggs, yolks, whisked *6*

Method

1. Wash and dry the chicken cubes. Add salt, dry fenugreek powder, ginger-garlic paste, green chillies and green coriander along with vinegar and mix thoroughly. Refrigerate for 15 minutes.

2. Heat oil in a pan, add gram flour and stir-fry till a pleasing aroma emanates. Add the chicken cubes and sauté on low heat for 3-5 minutes till the chicken is half cooked.

3. Add breadcrumbs and mix well. Remove and spread on a clean table top. Allow to cool.

4. Skewer the cubes 2" apart; roast in a tandoor/grill/oven. When done, move the cubes close together and coat with egg yolks.

5. Roast again till the egg yolk coating turns golden brown. Remove from the skewer and serve hot, garnished with onion rings.

CHICKEN SOYA KEBABS

Serves: 4-5   Preparation time: 45 minutes   Cooking time: 8-10 minutes

Ingredients

Chicken breasts, deboned,
skinned and cubed *4*
Lemon juice *15 ml / 1 tbsp*
Black pepper *(kali mirch)* powder
7 gm / 1½ tsp
Garlic *(lasan)* paste (p. 8) *10 gm / 2 tsp*
Salt *5 gm / 1 tsp*
Oil *15 ml / 1 tbsp*
Soya sauce *30 ml / 2 tbsp*
Butter/oil for basting

Method

1. Rub lemon juice on the chicken cubes and mix well. Keep aside for 30 minutes.

2. Pat the chicken cubes dry and sprinkle black pepper powder over them.

3. Mix garlic paste, salt, oil and soya sauce; add the chicken cubes and coat well. Marinate for 2-3 hours.

4. Preheat oven to 175 °C / 350 °F. Skewer chicken pieces 2 cm apart. Roast for 8-10 minutes or until cooked, basting once thoroughly.

CHICKEN SEEKH KEBABS

Serves: 4   Preparation time: 30 minutes   Cooking time: 6 minutes

Ingredients

Chicken, minced *1 kg / 5 cups*
Eggs *2*
Cumin *(jeera)* powder *15 gm / 1 tbsp*
Yellow chilli powder *5 gm / 1 tsp*
White pepper *(safed mirch)* powder
5 gm / 1 tsp
Salt to taste
Oil *20 ml / 4 tsp*
Cashewnuts *(kaju)*, pounded
60 gm / 4 tbsp
Ginger *(adrak)*, finely chopped
30 gm / 2 tbsp
Onions, finely chopped *20 gm / 4 tsp*
Green coriander *(hara dhaniya)*,
finely chopped *20 gm / 4 tsp*
Garam masala (p. 6) *5 gm / 1 tsp*
Oil for basting
Butter (unsalted) for brushing

Method

1. Whisk the eggs, add cumin powder, yellow chilli powder, white pepper powder, salt and 4 tsp oil. Add to the mince and mix well. Keep aside for 10 minutes.
2. Add cashewnuts, ginger, onions, coriander and garam masala. Mix well.
3. Divide into 10 equal portions.
4. Using wet hands, wrap two portions along each skewer. Keep 2" between each portion. Prepare 5 skewers like this.
5. Roast in a moderately hot tandoor or charcoal grill for about 6 minutes until golden brown in colour, or roast in a preheated oven at 150 °C / 300 °F for 8 minutes, basting with oil just once.
6. Remove from skewers and brush with butter.
7. Serve hot, garnished with onion rings and lemon wedges.

RESHMI KEBAB ZAFRANI

Minced chicken kababs on skewers

Serves: 4   Preparation time: 1 hour   Cooking time: 10 minutes

Ingredients

Chicken, minced *1 kg*
Eggs, whisked *2*
Cumin *(jeera)* powder *10 gm / 2 tsp*
Yellow chilli powder *5 gm / 1 tsp*
White pepper *(safed mirch)* powder
3 gm / ½ tsp
Salt to taste
Cashewnut *(kaju)* paste *45 gm*
Ginger *(adrak)* paste (p. 8)
20 gm / 4 tsp
Onion paste (p. 8) *20 gm / 4 tsp*
Garam masala (p. 6) *5 gm / 1 tsp*
Saffron *(kesar)* (in 2 tbsp warm milk)
a pinch

Green coriander *(hara dhaniya)*, chopped
20 gm / 4 tsp
Processed cheese, grated *100 gm*
Oil *20 ml / 4 tsp*

Method

1. Mix the chicken mince along with all the ingredients except oil and keep aside for 30 minutes.
2. Shape the chicken mince mixture along the length of skewers to shape into kebabs.
3. Cook in a tandoor for 6-8 minutes. Remove from tandoor, baste with oil and cook further for another 5 minutes or until brown.
4. Remove from skewers and serve hot.

COLOURFUL CHICKEN SEEKH KEBABS

Serves: 4-5   Preparation time: 20 minutes   Cooking time: 8-10 minutes

Ingredients

Chicken, minced *800 gm / 4 cups*
Eggs, whisked *2*
Cumin *(jeera)* powder *10 gm / 2 tsp*
Yellow chilli powder *5 gm / 1 tsp*
White pepper *(safed mirch)*
powder *5 gm / 1 tsp*
Salt to taste
Oil *45 ml / 3 tbsp*
Cashewnut *(kaju)* paste
45 gm / 3 tbsp
Garlic *(lasan)* paste (p. 8) *20 gm / 4 tsp*
Ginger *(adrak)*, chopped *20 gm / 4 tsp*
Green chillies, chopped *15 gm / 1 tbsp*
Green coriander *(hara dhaniya)*,
chopped *15 gm / 3 tsp*
Onion, chopped fine *10 gm / 2 tsp*
Cottage cheese *(paneer)* (p. 8),
grated *60 gm / 4 tbsp*

Garam masala (p. 6) *5 gm / 1 tsp*
Capsicum *(Shimla mirch)*, chopped fine *10 gm / 2 tsp*
Tomato, chopped fine *10 gm / 2 tsp*
Butter for basting *60 gm / 4 tbsp*
Chaat masala *5 gm / 1 tsp*
Lemon juice *30 ml / 2 tbsp*

Method

1. Add the whisked eggs, cumin powder, yellow chilli powder, white pepper powder, salt and oil to the minced chicken and mix well. Keep aside for 15 minutes.

2. Add the cashewnut and garlic pastes, ginger, green chillies, coriander, onions, cottage cheese and garam masala to the chicken mince and mix well.

3. Divide into 8 equal portions and make into balls.

Skewer the balls of mince. With wet hands spread the balls by pressing each along the length of the skewers to make 10 cm long kebabs, 4 cm apart.

4. Mix capsicum and tomato and press over skewers evenly from top to bottom.

5. Roast until golden brown in an oven at 175 °C / 350 °F for 8-10 minutes, basting with melted butter.

6. Sprinkle chaat masala and lemon juice and serve, garnished with onion rings and lemon wedges.

---— ❖ ---—

Away with Stains

Oven-to-table dishes can become stained while in the oven. Remove stain with a wet cloth and salt before putting the dish on the table.

---— ❖ ---—

MURGH CHANDNI KEBABS

(Chicken drumsticks stuffed with chicken-mince mixture and cooked in a tandoor)

Serves: 4   Preparation time: 2 hours 30 minutes   Cooking time: 15 minutes

Ingredients

Chicken drumsticks *16*
Chicken, minced *400 gm / 2 cups*
Green cardamom (*choti elaichi*)
powder *5 gm / 1 tsp*
Clove (*laung*) powder *2 gm / ¹/₃ tsp*
Salt to taste
Ginger-garlic *(adrak-lasan)* paste
(p. 8) *60 gm / 4 tbsp*
White pepper *(safed mirch)* powder
3 gm / ½ tsp
Egg, whisked *1*
Amul cheese, grated *100 gm / ½ cup*
Green chillies, chopped
25 gm / 5 tsp
Green coriander *(hara dhaniya)*,
chopped *20 gm / 4 tsp*
Cream *200 ml / 1 cup*

Nutmeg (*jaiphal*) and mace (*javitri*) powder *3 gm / ½ tsp*
Butter for basting *100 gm / ½ cup*

Method

1. Debone the chicken drumsticks and keep aside.
2. Mix the chicken mince with green cardamom and clove powders and salt. Fill the drumsticks with the mixture and seal with a toothpick.
3. Make a marinade with the remaining ingredients except butter and marinate the chicken drumsticks in it. Keep aside for 2 hours.
4. Skewer the drumsticks and cook in a tandoor for 10 minutes. Remove from tandoor/oven/grill, baste with butter and cook for another 2-5 minutes.
5. Remove from skewers; remove the toothpick. Wrap silver foil over one-third of the drumsticks and serve.

CREAMY CHICKEN TIKKAS

Serves: 4-6   Preparation time: 3 hours 45 minutes   Cooking time: 12 minutes

Ingredients

Chicken breasts, cubed *1 kg*
Ginger-garlic *(adrak-lasan)* paste
(p. 8) *60 gm / 4 tbsp*
Salt to taste
White pepper *(safed mirch)*
powder *5 gm / 1 tsp*
Egg, whisked *1*
Cheddar cheese, grated *60 gm / 4 tbsp*
Green chillies, deseeded and
finely chopped *8*
Green coriander *(hara dhaniya)*,
finely chopped *20 gm / 4 tsp*
Mace *(javitri)* and nutmeg *(jaiphal)*
powder *3 gm / ½ tsp*
Cornflour *(makkai ka atta)*
10 gm / 2 tsp
Cream *160 ml / ¾ cup*
Oil/butter for basting

Method

1. Rub ginger-garlic paste, salt and white pepper onto the chicken cubes. Keep aside for 15 minutes.
2. Add cheese, green chillies, coriander, mace-nutmeg powder, cornflour and cream to the whisked egg. Mix well and coat the chicken cubes with the prepared mixture. Marinate for at least 3 hours.
3. Skewer the chicken cubes 2 cm apart and roast in a preheated (137 °C / 275 °F) oven/grill/tandoor for 5-8 minutes. Hang skewers for 3-5 minutes to let excess liquid drip; brush with oil and roast again for 3 minutes.
4. Serve at once, garnished with chopped coriander, tomato slices and lemon wedges.

HONEY CHICKEN TIKKAS

Serves: 5 Preparation time: 3 hours 45 minutes Cooking time: 20 minutes

Ingredients

Chicken breasts, cleaned, deboned
1 kg
Lime juice *120 ml / ½ cup*
Honey *(shahad) 100 ml / ½ cup*
Red chilli powder *15 gm / 1 tbsp*
Garlic *(lasan)* paste (p. 8) *5 gm / 1 tsp*
White pepper *(safed mirch)*
powder *3 gm / ½ tsp*
Nutmeg *(jaiphal)* powder *3 gm / ½ tsp*
Red food colour *a pinch*
Salt to taste
Mustard oil *(sarson ka tel)*
30 gm / 2 tbsp

Method

1. Clean and debone the chicken breasts. Cut into 2" strips.

2. Combine all the ingredients, except mustard oil in a large bowl; coat chicken strips evenly and leave to marinate for 3 hours.

3. Skewer chicken strips 2 cm apart; grill / bake / roast in a charcoal grill / oven / tandoor for 8-10 minutes, basting occasionally with mustard oil. Serve hot, garnished with onion rings and tomato slices.

TANGRI KEBABS HARYALI

(Mint and coriander-flavoured kebabs)

Serves: 4   Preparation time: 3 hours   Cooking time: 15 minutes

Ingredients

Chicken drumsticks *12*
Ginger *(adrak)* paste (p. 8) *20 gm / 4 tsp*
Garlic *(lasan)* paste (p. 8) *15 gm / 1 tbsp*
Salt to taste
Lemon juice *15 ml / 1 tbsp*
Yoghurt *(dahi)* (p. 6), hung
100 gm / ½ cup
Mint *(pudina)*, finely
chopped *30 gm / 2 tbsp*
Green coriander *(hara dhaniya)*,
finely chopped *50 gm / ¼ cup*
Garam masala (p. 6) *5 gm / 1 tsp*
Coriander *(dhaniya)* powder
5 gm / 1 tsp
Cumin *(jeera)* powder *5 gm / 1 tsp*
Oil *60 ml / 4 tbsp*

Dry fenugreek *(kasoori methi)* powder *5 gm / 1 tsp*
Green chillies, finely chopped *15 gm / 1 tbsp*
Butter for basting

Method

1. Marinate the chicken drumsticks with ginger paste, garlic paste, salt and lemon juice. Keep aside for 30 minutes.

2. Mix all the other ingredients and marinate the drumsticks with the prepared mixture. Keep aside for two and a half hours.

3. Skewer the drumsticks and cook in a tandoor/grill/oven for 8-10 minutes.

4. Remove from tandoor/grill/oven, baste with butter and cook further for 5 minutes or until done.

5. Remove from skewers and serve hot.

NEZA KEBABS

(Marinated chicken legs with a distinctive flavour of green cardamoms)

Serves: 4   Preparation time: 40 minutes   Cooking time: 25 minutes

Ingredients

Chicken, legs *900 gm*
Ginger-garlic *(adrak-lasan)* paste
(p. 8) *80 gm / 5 ¹/₃ tbsp*
Salt *8 gm / 1 ¹/₂ tsp*
White pepper *(safed mirch)* powder
4 gm / ³/₄ tsp
Garam masala (p. 6) *4 gm / ³/₄ tsp*
Dry fenugreek *(kasoori methi)*
powder *2 gm / ¹/₃ tsp*
Vinegar *(sirka) 20 ml / 4 tsp*
Green coriander *(hara dhaniya),*
chopped *40 gm / 2 ²/₃ tbsp*
Green cardamom *(choti elaichi)*
powder *4 gm / ³/₄ tsp*
Oil *60 ml / 4 tbsp*

Gram flour *(besan) 300 gm / 1 ¹/₂ cups*
Eggs, whisked *4*
Cream *200 gm / 1 cup*
Butter for basting

Method

1. Wash and clean the chicken legs.
2. Prepare a marinade by mixing together ginger-garlic paste, salt, white pepper powder, garam masala, dry fenugreek powder, vinegar, green coriander and green cardamom powder. Marinate the chicken legs in this marinade for 20 minutes.
3. Heat oil in a pan; add gram flour and stir-fry on low heat till a pleasing smell emanates. Remove from heat and transfer to a mixing bowl. Allow to cool.

4. Add 1 egg and blend to make a smooth paste; add cream and mix well.

5. Add the remaining eggs to the mixture and mix thoroughly. Coat the chicken legs with this marinade and keep aside for 20 minutes.

6. Skewer the chicken legs. Cook in a tandoor / oven / grill for about 8-10 minutes or till slightly coloured. Remove and let excess liquids drip.

7. Baste lightly with butter and roast again for 2-3 minutes or till completely done.

8. Remove from skewers onto a serving platter. Serve, garnished with lemon wedges, cucumber and tomato dices and onion rings.

Jar Firmly

Store leftover egg whites in a screw-top jar. They will keep for 7-10 days in the fridge.

SARSON KE TIKKE

(Mustard-flavoured roasted chicken cubes)

Serves: 4   Preparation time: 4 hours 30 minutes   Cooking time: 15-20 minutes

Ingredients

Chicken drumsticks, boneless,
cut into pieces *900 gm*
Lemon juice *100 ml / ½ cup*
Salt to taste
Ginger-garlic *(adrak-lasan)* paste
(p. 8) *60 gm / 4 tbsp*
Green coriander *(hara dhaniya)*,
chopped *100 gm / ½ cup*
Garlic *(lasan)*, chopped *75 gm / 5 tbsp*
Green chillies, chopped *45 gm / 3 tbsp*
Yellow chilli paste *15 gm / 1 tbsp*
Mustard *(rai)* paste *45 gm / 3 tbsp*
Mustard oil *(sarson ka tel)*
120 ml / ½ cup
Gram flour *(besan) 60 gm / 4 tbsp*
Garam masala (p. 6) *10 gm / 2 tsp*
Butter *60 gm / 4 tbsp*

Method

1. Apply lemon juice, salt and ginger-garlic paste evenly on the chicken pieces.
2. Make a paste by blending together green coriander, garlic and green chillies. To this add all the other ingredients except butter.
3. Squeeze the chicken pieces and add to the prepared paste. Mix well and keep aside for 3-4 hours.
4. Skewer the chicken pieces and cook in a tandoor or charcoal grill for 10 minutes.
5. Remove, baste with butter and cook further until done.
6. Remove from skewers and serve hot.

FISH TIKKAS

Serves: 4-6   Preparation time: 1 hour 30 minutes   Cooking time: 30 minutes

Ingredients

Fish fillets, cut into cubes *1 kg*
Salt to taste
Lemon juice *15 ml / 1 tbsp*
Yoghurt *(dahi)* (p. 6) *120 gm / ½ cup*
Vinegar *(sirka) 15 ml / 1 tbsp*
Garam masala (p. 6) *15 gm / 1 tbsp*
Cumin *(jeera)* seeds, ground
10 gm / 2 tsp
Carom *(ajwain)* seeds *3 gm / ½ tsp*
Red chilli powder *5 gm / 1 tsp*
Garlic *(lasan)* paste (p. 8) *10 gm / 2 tsp*
Oil / butter for basting

Method

1. Wash and dry the cubed fish fillets. Sprinkle salt and lemon juice. Set aside to marinate for half an hour.
2. In a bowl, combine yoghurt with the remaining ingredients and whisk well. Pour mixture over the fish cubes and coat evenly. Leave to marinate for at least one hour.
3. Preheat oven to 175 °C / 350 °F.
4. Roast, bake or grill till the fillets are golden brown in colour and cooked through, basting just once.
5. Serve hot.

MAHI TIKKAS

(Buttered fish tikkas)

Serves: 4   Preparation time: 2 hours 30 minutes   Cooking time: 15-20 minutes

Ingredients

Fish, cut into boneless pieces *1 kg*
Clarified butter (*ghee*) *100 gm / ½ cup*
Onions, sliced *120 gm / ½ cup*
Garlic *(lasan)*, chopped *45 gm / 3 tbsp*
Salt to taste
Red chilli powder *30 gm / 2 tbsp*
Coriander (*dhaniya*) powder
30 gm / 2 tbsp
Cumin (*jeera*) powder *5 gm / 1 tsp*
Turmeric (*haldi*) powder
5 gm / 1 tsp
Yoghurt *(dahi)* (p. 6) *100 gm / ½ cup*
Butter for basting

Method

1. In a pan, heat clarified butter and fry the onions till brown. Remove, drain excess clarified butter and blend to make a paste.

2. In the same pan, fry the garlic and keep aside.

3. Allow the clarified butter to cool. Mix the onion paste, garlic, all the other ingredients and the fish pieces with the clarified butter and keep aside for 2 hours.

4. Skewer the fish pieces and roast in a tandoor/oven/grill for 5-10 minutes. Remove, baste with butter and cook further for 3-5 minutes.

5. Remove from skewers and serve hot.

YAM KEBABS

Serves: 4   Preparation time: 20 minutes   Cooking time: 20 minutes

Ingredients

Yam *(jimikand)* 1½ kg
Green chillies, finely chopped
5 gm / 1 tsp
Ginger *(adrak)*, finely chopped
5 gm / 1 tsp
Salt 8 gm / 1½ tsp
White pepper *(safed mirch)* powder
5 gm / 1 tsp
Red chilli powder 5 gm / 1 tsp
Chaat masala 5 gm / 1 tsp
Green coriander *(hara dhaniya)*,
finely chopped
5 gm / 1 tsp
Breadcrumbs 100 gm / ½ cup
Oil 150 ml / ¾ cup

Method

1. Peel and wash the yam. Immerse in boiling water and cook until it becomes tender.
2. Remove from water, grate finely and squeeze out all the excess water.
3. Add the remaining ingredients to the grated yam. Mix well and divide into 8 equal portions. Shape the portions into medallions.
4. Shallow fry on medium heat till they become crisp and golden brown on both sides.
5. Serve hot.

SUBZI KE SEEKH

(Skewered vegetable pieces)

Serves: 4   Preparation time: 1 hour   Cooking time: 10 minutes

Ingredients

Potatoes *4*
Yam *(jimikand) 500 gm*
Cauliflower *(phool gobi) 100 gm*
Beans *(sem)*, finely chopped
100 gm / ½ cup
Carrots *(gajar)*, finely chopped
100 gm / ½ cup
Cottage cheese *(paneer)* (p. 8),
mashed *125 gm / ½ cup*
Cashewnuts *(kaju)*, ground
60 gm / 4 tbsp
Ginger *(adrak)* paste (p. 8) *10 gm / 2 tsp*
Garlic *(lasan)* paste (p. 8) *10 gm / 2 tsp*
Onions, minced *120 gm / ½ cup*
Green chillies, minced *15 gm / 1 tbsp*
Red chilli powder *5 gm / 1 tsp*

Cumin *(jeera)* seeds, roasted *5 gm / 1 tsp*
Green coriander *(hara dhaniya)*, minced *30 gm / 2 tbsp*
Salt to taste
Oil for basting

Method

1. Boil the potatoes and yam in sufficient water until tender. Remove skins and mash finely.
2. Mix together all the ingredients along with mashed potatoes and yam. Knead to a stiff dough and keep aside for 30 minutes.
3. Spread the mixture along the length of the skewers to shape into kebabs.
4. Cook in a tandoor/oven/grill for 10 minutes.
5. Remove, baste with oil and cook for 5 minutes.
6. Remove from skewers and serve hot.

COTTAGE CHEESE TIKKAS

Serves: 4-5   Preparation time: 2 hours 15 minutes   Cooking time: 10 minutes

Ingredients

Cottage cheese *(paneer)* (p. 8) *1 kg*
Caraway seeds *(shahi jeera)*
3 gm / ½ tsp
White pepper *(safed mirch)* powder
5 gm / 1 tsp
Garam masala (p. 6) *10 gm / 2 tsp*
Turmeric *(haldi)* powder *5 gm / 1 tsp*
Lemon juice *25 ml / 5 tsp*
Salt to taste
Cream *150 ml / ¾ cup*
Yoghurt *(dahi)* (p. 6), hung
150 gm / ¾ cup
Gram flour *(besan)* / cornflour
(makkai ka atta) 30 gm / 2 tbsp
Fenugreek *(methi)* powder
5 gm / 1 tsp
Garlic *(lasan)* paste (p. 8)
15 gm / 1 tbsp

Ginger *(adrak)* paste (p. 8) *15 gm / 1 tbsp*
Red chilli powder *10 gm / 2 tsp*
Saffron *(kesar) 3 gm / ½ tsp*
Cottage cheese *(paneer)* (p. 8), grated *60 gm / 4 tbsp*
Butter to baste *50 gm / ¼ cup*
Chaat masala *10 gm / 2 tsp*

Method

1. Wash and cut the paneer into small cubes (30 pieces).
2. Mix the caraway seeds, white pepper powder, garam masala, turmeric powder, two-thirds of the lemon juice and salt. Sprinkle over the paneer cubes. Keep aside for 1 hour in the refrigerator.
3. Mix cream, yoghurt and gram flour / cornflour in a bowl. Add the remaining ingredients and whisk well to make a fine batter.

4. Add the paneer cubes to this and marinate for at least 1 hour.
5. Preheat the oven to 150-175 °C / 300-350 °F).
6. Thread the paneer cubes onto the skewers, 2 cm apart.

7. Roast in an oven/tandoor/charcoal grill for 5-6 minutes. Baste with melted butter.
8. Sprinkle with chaat masala and the remaining lemon juice. Serve with a green salad.

———— ❖ ————

Lime-n-Lemony

Put a lemon in hot water before squeezing it.
You will get more juice out of it.

———— ❖ ————

MUSHROOM CUTLETS

Serves: 3-4   Preparation time: 30 minutes   Cooking time: 15-20 minutes

Ingredients

Mushrooms *(guchi)*, chopped
150 gm / ³/₄ cup
Potatoes, boiled, deskinned *3*
Peas *(mattar)*, boiled 50 gm / ¹/₄ cup
Onions, finely chopped *3*
Green chillies, finely chopped *3*
Ginger *(adrak)*, finely chopped
5 gm / 1 tsp
Fresh coconut *(nariyal)*, grated
15 gm / 1 tbsp
Red chilli powder 5 gm / 1 tsp
Turmeric *(haldi)* powder 3 gm / ¹/₂ tsp
Coriander *(dhaniya)* leaves, chopped
15 gm / 1 tbsp
Salt to taste
Breadcrumbs 3 gm / 2 tbsp
Gram flour *(besan)* 100 gm / ¹/₂ cup

Method

1. Mix chopped mushrooms, potatoes and peas together.

2. Add chopped onions, green chillies, ginger, grated coconut, red chilli powder, turmeric and coriander. Mix well and season with salt. Lastly add coarsely pounded breadcrumbs.

3. Put gram flour in a large bowl. Add water and a pinch of salt to make a batter of coating consistency. Mix thoroughly.

4. Shape the mushroom mixture into flat round cutlets.

5. Heat oil in a frying pan. When it starts smoking, dip each cutlet lightly in the gram flour batter and fry till crisp and golden brown on each side. Serve hot.

SESAME-SEED, COTTAGE CHEESE KEBABS

Serves: 4   Preparation time: 30 minutes   Cooking time: 15 minutes

Ingredients

Cottage cheese *(paneer)* (p. 8),
finely grated *500 gm / 2 ½ cups*
Green cardamom *(choti elaichi)*
powder *3 gm / ½ tsp*
Garam masala (p. 6) *10 gm / 2 tsp*
Green chillies, chopped *5 gm / 1 tsp*
Green coriander *(hara dhaniya)*,
chopped *10 gm / 2 tsp*
Mace *(javitri)* powder *3 gm / ½ tsp*
Salt to taste
Onions, finely chopped *100 gm / ½ cup*
White pepper *(safed mirch)* powder
5 gm / 1 tsp
Yellow or red chilli powder *6 gm / 1 tsp*
Yoghurt *(dahi)* (p. 6), hung
400 gm / 2 cups
Gram flour *(besan)* / cornflour
(makkai ka atta) 60 gm / 4 tbsp
Egg white (optional) *1*

Sesame seeds *(til)* (optional) *100 gm / ½ cup*
Oil *100 ml / ½ cup*

Method

1. Combine all the ingredients except the gram flour/ cornflour and sesame seeds in a bowl. Mix with a wooden spoon.

2. Add the gram flour/cornflour and mix for 2 minutes.

3. Divide the mixture into 20 equal portions. Make each portion into a round ball, roll it in your palm and press slightly to get a 4 cm-round patty.

4. Cool the cutlets in the refrigerator for 20 minutes.

5. Heat the oil in a deep pan or a wok *(kadhai)*. Fry until golden crisp. Alternatively, lightly coat each cutlet with egg white, sprinkle with sesame seeds and shallow fry in a non-stick pan.

6. Serve with cucumber, tomato and onion slices.

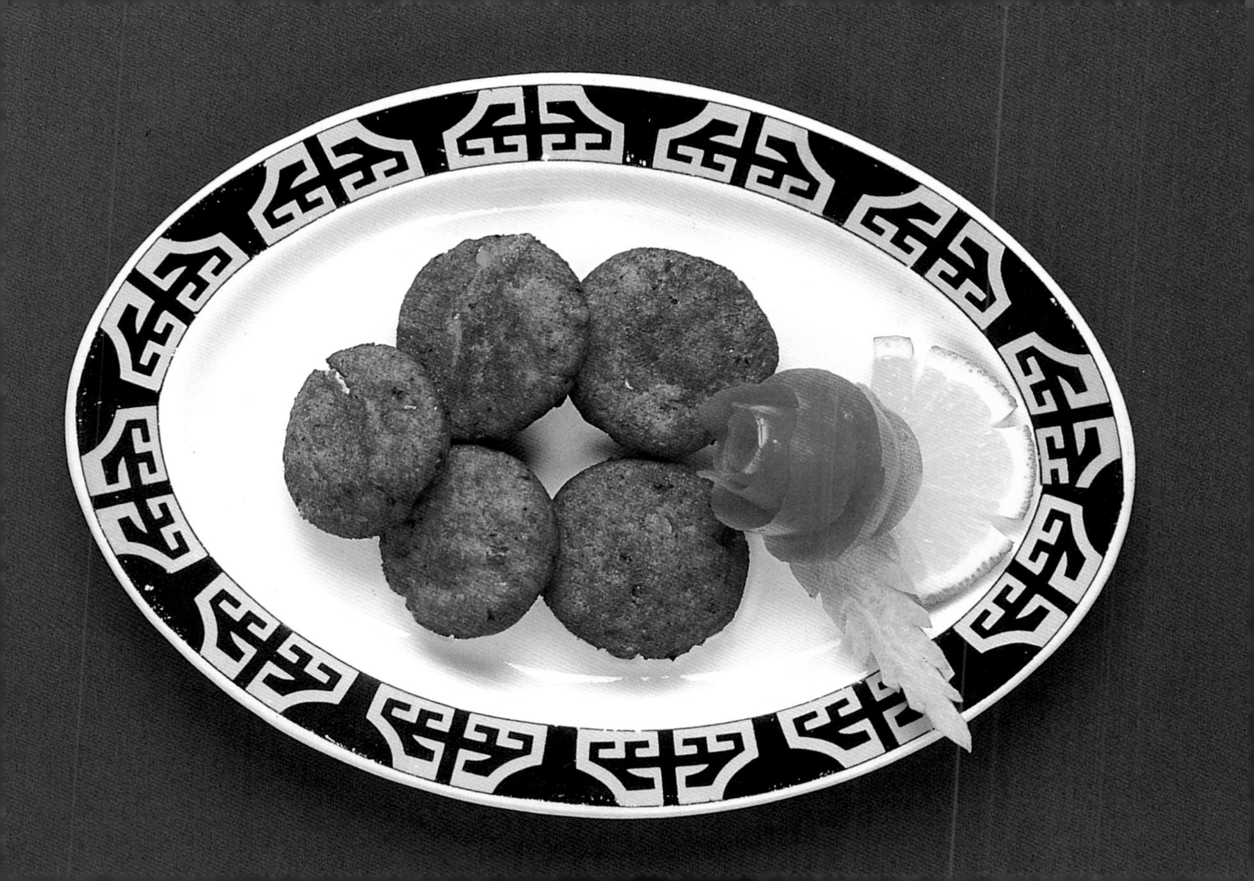

KASTOORI PANEER TIKKAS

(Cottage cheese cubes flavoured with fenugreek)

Serves: 4   Preparation time: 2 hours 15 minutes   Cooking time: 10 minutes

Ingredients

Cottage cheese *(paneer)* (p. 8) *1 kg*
Caraway seeds *(shahi jeera)*
3 gm / ²/₃ tsp
White pepper *(safed mirch)* powder
5 gm / 1 tsp
Garam masala (p. 6) *10 gm / 2 tsp*
Lemon juice *25 ml / 5 tsp*
Salt to taste
Cottage cheese *(paneer)* (p. 8), grated
50 gm / ¼ cup
Cream *100 gm / ½ cup*
Yoghurt *(dahi)* (p. 6), drained
150 gm / ¾ cup
Gram flour *(besan)* / cornflour
(makkai ka atta) 30 gm / 2 tbsp

Dry fenugreek *(kasoori methi)* leaves *20 gm / 4 tsp*
Garlic *(lasan)* paste (p. 8) *15 gm / 3 tsp*
Ginger *(adrak)* paste (p. 8) *15 gm / 3 tsp*
Red chilli powder *10 gm / 2 tsp*
Butter to baste *50 gm / ¼ cup*
Chaat masala (optional) *10 gm / 2 tsp*

Method

1. Wash and cut the cottage cheese into 4 cm cubes (30 pieces).

2. Mix the caraway seeds, white pepper, garam masala, two-thirds of the lemon juice and salt together. Add the grated cottage cheese to this mixture. Marinate and keep in the refrigerator for 1 hour.

3. Mix the cream, yoghurt, gram flour / cornflour and dry fenugreek in a bowl.
4. Add the remaining ingredients to this mixture and whisk to a fine batter.
5. Then add the cottage cheese cubes and leave aside for at least 1 hour.
6. Preheat oven to 150-175 °C / 300-350 °F.

7. Skewer cottage cheese cubes, 2 cm apart.
8. Roast in an oven / tandoor / charcoal grill for 5-6 minutes.
9. Baste with melted butter. Sprinkle chaat masala and the remaining lemon juice. Serve with slices of cucumbers, tomatoes, onions and chutney.

———— ❖ ————

Butter Blues

To quickly thaw butter stored in a refrigerator,
run some tap water over it.

———— ❖ ————

PANEER-PUDINA TIKKAS

(Cottage cheese tikkas stuffed with mint, coriander and green chillies)

Serves: 4   Preparation time: 40 minutes   Cooking time: 10 minutes

Ingredients

Cottage cheese (*paneer*) (p. 8) *800 gm*
Red chilli powder *5 gm / 1 tsp*
Turmeric (*haldi*) powder *5 gm / 1 tsp*
Salt to taste, Lemons *5*
Chaat masala *5 gm / 1 tsp*
Garam masala (p. 6) *10 gm / 2 tsp*
Mint (*pudina*) leaves, chopped
75 gm / 5 tbsp
Green coriander (*hara dhaniya*),
chopped *75 gm / 5 tbsp*
Green chillies, chopped *25 gm / 5 tsp*
Yoghurt (*dahi*) (p. 6) *250 gm / 1¼ cups*
Ginger (*adrak*), chopped *15 gm / 1 tbsp*
Ginger-garlic (*adrak-lasan*) paste
(p. 8) *60 gm / 4 tbsp*
Yellow chilli powder *25 gm / 5 tsp*

Carom (*ajwain*) seeds *10 gm / 2 tsp*
Butter *60 gm / 4 tbsp*
White pepper (*safed mirch*) powder *5 gm / 1 tsp*

Method

1. Cube the cottage cheese into squares. Sprinkle red chilli and turmeric powder and salt; keep aside.
2. Add lemon juice, half the chaat masala and garam masala and mix well.
3. Slit the cottage cheese cubes and fill with the chopped mint, coriander and green chillies.
4. Whisk yoghurt with the remaining ingredients. Coat the cubes evenly with this mixture.
5. Skewer the cubes and cook on a charcoal grill.
6. Remove from skewers; sprinkle the remaining chaat masala and garam masala and serve.

PANEER-SABU DANA KE KEBAB

(Cottage cheese and sago croquettes)

Serves: 4   Preparation time: 1 hour   Cooking time: 15 minutes

Ingredients

Cottage cheese (*paneer*) (p. 8) *500 gm*
Sago (*sabu dana*) *100 gm / ½ cup*
Spring onions, minced *100 gm / ½ cup*
Green chillies, chopped *10 gm / 2 tsp*
Cashewnuts (*kaju*), broken
45 gm / 3 tbsp
Large raisins (*sultanas*) *60 gm / 4 tbsp*
Cumin (*jeera*) seeds, roasted
5 gm / 1 tsp
Turmeric (*haldi*) powder
3 gm / ½ tsp
Garam masala (p. 6) *5 gm / 1 tsp*
Cornflour (*makkai ka atta*)
30 gm / 2 tbsp
Salt to taste
Oil for frying

Method

1. Mash the cottage cheese and heat. When it leaves water, squeeze and mash again.

2. Boil sago pellets and drain. Blend to break into smaller lumps without making into a paste.

3. Mix together all the ingredients along with mashed cottage cheese and sago, and knead. Keep aside for half an hour.

4. Shape into flat round cutlets. Heat a griddle (*tawa*), brush with oil and fry the cutlets, a few at a time, until golden brown in colour.

5. Remove, drain excess oil and serve hot.

GRILLED COTTAGE CHEESE ROLLS

Serves: 4   Preparation: 10 minutes   Cooking: 20 minutes

Ingredients

Cottage cheese *(paneer)*, in a firm
block *500 gm*
For the stuffing:
Cottage cheese *(paneer)* (p. 8),
grated *150 gm / ¾ cup*
Oil *75 ml / 5 tbsp*
Mushrooms *(guchi)*, chopped
150 gm / ¾ cup
Capsicum (Shimla *mirch*), chopped
150 gm / ¾ cup
Onions, chopped *150 gm / ¾ cup*
Coconut *(nariyal)* powder
100 gm / ½ cup
Cottage cheese *(paneer)* (p. 8),
grated *150 gm / ¾ cup*
Potatoes, boiled, grated *100 gm / ½ cup*

Caraway seeds *(shahi jeera) 5 gm / 1 tsp*
Cayenne pepper *10 gm / 2 tsp*
Dry fenugreek *(kasoori methi) 5 gm / 1 tsp*
White pepper *(safed mirch)* powder *20 gm / 4 tsp*
Turmeric *(haldi)* powder *5 gm / 1 tsp*
Raisins *(kishmish) 100 gm / ½ cup*
Lemon juice *10 ml / 2 tsp*, Salt to taste
For the coating:
Gram flour *(besan) 50 gm / ¼ cup*
Water *20 ml / 4 tsp*
Cornflour *(makkai ka atta) 100 gm / ½ cup*
Cream *100 gm / ½ cup*
Saffron *(kesar) ½ gm / a pinch*
Green coriander *(hara dhaniya)*, chopped *20 gm / 4 tsp*

Method

1. Slice cottage cheese lengthwise into 15 x 6 x 0.5 cm pieces.

2. Heat oil, sauté mushrooms, capsicum, onions and coconut powder. Add grated cottage cheese along with other ingredients for the stuffing. Stir-fry for a few seconds and remove from heat.

3. Mix gram flour with just enough water to make a thick paste. Spread the paste on one side of the cottage cheese slices, turn over, spread 3 tsp of the filling and shape into rolls. Keep aside.

4. Add the remaining ingredients for the coating to the gram flour-water paste. Coat the cottage cheese rolls evenly and bake in an oven for 10-12 minutes at low heat.

5. Sprinkle with chaat masala. Garnish with grated carrots and lemon wedges.

The Cutting Edge of Cornflour

*Fritters (pakodas) turn out crisper and tastier if
a little cornflour is added to the gram flour
while mixing the dough.*

ZAFRANI MALAI PANEER TIKKAS

(Saffron and cheese-flavoured cottage cheese cubes)

Serves: 4   Preparation time: 1 hour   Cooking time: 15 minutes

Ingredients

Cottage cheese *(paneer)* (p. 8) *1 kg*
Salt to taste
White pepper *(safed mirch)* powder
4 gm / 1 tsp
Lemon juice *100 ml / ½ cup*
Cheddar cheese *100 gm*
Cream *60 gm / 4 tbsp*
Green chillies, deseeded,
chopped *3*
Saffron *(kesar) 1 gm / a pinch*
Oil for basting

Method

1. Cut cottage cheese into 20 even-sized cubes.
2. Apply salt, pepper and lemon juice and keep aside for 15 minutes.
3. Grate Cheddar cheese in a bowl; whisk in the cream to make a fine paste. Add green chillies.
4. Soak saffron strands in 30 ml hot water for 10 minutes. Add to the cream mixture.
6. Drain the cottage cheese cubes and marinate in the cream mixture for 45 minutes.
7. Skewer the cottage cheese and roast in a preheated oven at 135 °C / 275 °F for 12 minutes, basting occasionally. Serve with green salad and chutney.

KEBAB-E-CHAMAN

(Spinach and potato cutlets)

Serves: 4   Preparation time: 1 hour   Cooking time: 15 minutes

Ingredients

Spinach *(palak)* 1 kg
Potatoes *400 gm*
Bengal gram *(chana dal)*
150 gm / ³/₄ cup
Green chillies, chopped *25 gm / 5 tsp*
Ginger *(adrak)*, chopped *25 gm / 5 tsp*
Green coriander *(hara dhaniya)*
25 gm / 5 tsp
Raisins *(kishmish)*, finely cut
100 gm / ¹/₂ cup
Cumin *(jeera)* powder *20 gm / 4 tsp*
Coriander *(dhaniya)* powder
15 gm / 1 tbsp
Dry fenugreek *(kasoori methi)*
powder *10 gm / 2 tsp*
Garam masala (p. 6) *10 gm / 2 tsp*
Salt to taste

Cashewnuts *(kaju)*, finely chopped *100 gm / ¹/₂ cup*
Clarified butter *(ghee) 150 gm / ³/₄ cup*

Method

1. Boil the spinach, potatoes and Bengal gram separately.

2. Chop the spinach finely, mash the potatoes and Bengal gram.

3. Mix the green chillies, ginger and green coriander with the mashed potatoes and Bengal gram, along with spinach and all the other ingredients except clarified butter. Shape into flat round cutlets.

4. Heat a griddle *(tawa)* and shallow fry the cutlets in clarified butter until crisp and golden brown on both sides.

5. Remove, drain excess clarified butter and serve hot.

CAULIFLOWER KEBABS

Serves: 4   Preparation time: 15 minutes   Cooking time: 15 minutes

Ingredients

Cauliflower *(phool gobi) 400 gm*
Potatoes *200 gm*
Breadcrumbs, fresh *60 gm / 4 tbsp*
Red chilli powder *5 gm / 1 tsp*
Salt to taste
Chaat masala *5 gm / 1 tsp*
Green chillies, finely chopped
5 gm / 1 tsp
Green coriander *(hara dhaniya)*,
finely chopped *5 gm / 1 tsp*
Ginger *(adrak)*, chopped *5 gm / 1 tsp*
Oil *150 ml / ¾ cup*

Method

1. Boil the cauliflower and potatoes separately. Drain excess water and allow to cool. Grate them separately.
2. Mix the grated cauliflower and grated potatoes with the breadcrumbs, red chilli powder, salt, chaat masala, green chillies, green coriander and ginger.
3. Divide into 16 equal portions and shape into medallions.
4. Heat a griddle *(tawa)*. Brush with oil and shallow fry the medallions, a few at a time, until golden brown.
5. Drain excess oil and serve hot.

STUFFED POTATO CUTLETS

Serves: 4   Preparation time: 30 minutes   Cooking time: 30 minutes

Ingredients

Potatoes, boiled, mashed
400 gm / 2 cups
Breadcrumbs, fresh *25 gm / 5 tsp*
White pepper *(safed mirch)* powder
3 gm / ½ tsp
Salt *5 gm / 1 tsp*
Green chillies, chopped *5 gm / 1 tsp*
Green coriander *(hara dhaniya)*,
chopped *5 gm / 1 tsp*
Ginger *(adrak)*, chopped
3 gm / ½ tsp
Large raisins *(sultanas)*, chopped
45 gm / 3 tbsp
Oil *75 ml / 5 tbsp*

Method

1. Add breadcrumbs, white pepper powder, salt, green chillies, green coriander and ginger to the mashed potatoes.

2. Mix well and divide into 8 equal portions.

3. Divide the chopped raisins also into 8 equal portions.

4. Stuff each portion of the chopped raisins into one portion of the potato mixture and shape into medallions.

5. Heat a griddle *(tawa)*. Brush with oil and shallow fry the medallions until golden brown.

6. Drain excess oil and serve.

COTTAGE CHEESE CROQUETTES

Serves: 4   Preparation time: 10 minutes   Cooking time: 15 minutes

Ingredients

Cottage cheese *(paneer)* (p. 8),
grated *500 gm / 2 ½ cups*
Green chillies, chopped *4*
Green coriander *(hara dhaniya)*,
chopped *15 gm / 1 tbsp*
White pepper *(safed mirch)*
5 gm / 1 tsp
Red chilli powder *5 gm /1 tsp*
Carom *(ajwain)* seeds *3 gm / ½ tsp*
Egg (optional) *1*
Garam masala (p. 6) *5 gm / 1 tsp*
Oil for frying
Gram flour *(besan) 75 gm / 5 tbsp*

Method

1. Combine grated cottage cheese and all other ingredients, adding gram flour in the end, and mix together in a bowl to make a smooth paste.
2. Shape the mixture into round croquettes/cutlets.
3. Heat oil in a wok *(kadhai)* till it starts smoking. Slide a few cutlets/croquettes at a time into the oil and fry till they are golden brown and crisp on all sides.
4. Serve hot.

ANJEER KI CHUTNEY

(Fig chutney)

Serves: 4   Preparation time: 30 minutes   Cooking time: 30 minutes

Ingredients

Figs *(anjeer)*, dried *500 gm / 2 ½ cups*
Almonds *(badam) 60 gm / ¼ cup*
Oil *100 ml / ½ cup*
Onions, chopped *100 gm / ½ cup*
Garlic *(lasan)*, chopped
100 gm / ½ cup
Sugar *60 gm / 4 tbsp*
Red chilli powder *5 gm / 1 tsp*
Green chillies, chopped *15 gm / 1 tbsp*
Salt to taste
Malt vinegar *(sirka) 60 ml / 4 tbsp*
White vinegar *(sirka) 25 ml / 5 tsp*
Green cardamom *(choti elaichi)*
powder *10 gm / 2 tsp*
Melon *(magaz)* seeds *10 gm / 2 tsp*

Method

1. Blanch the figs and almonds in water for 10 minutes and keep aside. Fry the onions and garlic in oil until golden brown. Remove and drain.

2. Blend all the ingredients except green cardamom powder and melon seeds to make a paste.

3. Transfer to a bowl and garnish with green cardamom powder and melon seeds.

4. Refrigerate and use as required (can be stored in an airtight container in a refrigerator for 1-2 months).

MIXED PICKLE

Preparation time: 7 days   Cooking time: 20 minutes

Ingredients

Cauliflower *(phool gobi)* ½ *kg*
Turnips *300 gm*
Carrots *(gajar)* *300 gm*
Mustard oil *(sarson ka tel)*
350 ml / 1¾ cups
Onions, puréed *100 gm / 1½ cups*
Ginger-garlic *(adrak-lasan)* paste
(p. 8) *60 gm / ¼ cup*
Sugar *200 gm / 1 cup*
Vinegar *(sirka)* *200 ml / 1 cup*
Garam masala (p. 6) *25 gm / 5 tsp*
Red chilli powder *20 gm / 4 tsp*
Cumin *(jeera)* seeds *20 gm / 4 tsp*
Mustard *(rai)* seeds *20 gm / 4 tsp*
Salt to taste

Method

1. Cut the cauliflower into florets, turnips and carrots into thin slices. Dry in the sun for two days.
2. Heat mustard oil in a wok *(kadhai)*. Add onion purée and ginger-garlic paste and stir-fry for a few minutes.
3. Dissolve sugar in vinegar and keep aside.
4. Stir in the dry spices along with salt to taste and the vegetables. Cover and cook for 5-10 minutes.
5. Add the vinegar mixture to the vegetables and mix well. Remove from heat and allow to cool.
6. Transfer into a glass jar and cover with a cloth. Keep in the sun for 5 days. Serve as an accompaniment with any meal.

PUDINA PARANTHA

(Wholewheat bread flavoured with mint)

Serves: 4   Preparation time: 30 minutes   Cooking time: 10 minutes

Ingredients

Wholewheat flour (*atta*)
½ kg / 2 ½ cups
Salt *5 gm / 1 tsp*
Clarified butter (*ghee*)
120 gm / ½ cup
Water *250 ml / 1 ¼ cups*
Mint (*pudina*) leaves, dried
5 gm / 1 tsp

Method

1. Mix flour, salt and half of clarified butter; add water and knead to a smooth dough. Cover and keep aside for 30 minutes.

3. Shape the dough into a ball. Flatten into a round disc with a rolling pin. Apply the remaining clarified butter and sprinkle dried mint leaves.

4. Pleat the dough into 1 collected strip. Shape into balls and roll out into 6"-diameter pancakes.

5. Heat a griddle (*tawa*)/tandoor and cook till brown spots appear on both the sides.

Taftan

Khasta Roti

Pudina Parantha

Missi Roti

TAFTAN

(Rich, leavened, rice-flour bread)

Serves: 4   Preparation time: 1 hour
Cooking time: 10 minutes

Ingredients

Rice flour (*chawal ka atta*) *480 gm / 2 ½ cups*
Salt to taste, Water
Sugar *3 gm / ½ tsp*
Milk *240 ml / 1 cup*
Clarified butter (*ghee*) *180 gm / ³/₄ cup*
Yeast *3 gm / ½ tsp*
Melon *(magaz)* seeds *10 gm / 2 tsp*
Green coriander (*hara dhaniya*),
chopped *10 gm / 2 tsp*

Method

1. Sieve flour and salt together.
2. Make a well in the flour. Add water, sugar, milk, clarified butter, yeast and melon seeds. Mix gradually and knead into a soft dough.

3. Divide into 4 equal balls and set aside for half an hour.
4. Dust lightly and roll into 3 ½" discs, ¼" thick. Sprinkle with coriander.
5. Bake in a tandoor till brown.
6. Brush with clarified butter and serve hot.

MISSI ROTI

(Flavoured gram-flour bread cooked in a tandoor)

Serves: 4   Preparation time: 30 minutes
Cooking time: 10 minutes

Ingredients

Gram flour (*besan*) *300 gm / 1 ½ cups*
Flour (*maida*) *100 gm / ½ cup*
Green chillies, chopped *25 gm / 5 tsp*
Ginger (*adrak*), chopped *25 gm / 5 tsp*

Green coriander (*hara dhaniya*),
chopped *25 gm / 5 tsp*
Pomegranate seeds (*anardana*), *20 gm / 4 tsp*
Cumin (*jeera*) seeds *15 gm / 1 tbsp*
Onion seeds (*kalonji*) *25 gm / 5 tsp*
Salt *10 gm / 2 tsp*
Butter *100 gm / ½ cup*
Clarified butter (*ghee*) *30 gm / 2 tbsp*

Method

1. Chop green chillies, ginger and coriander finely.
2. Crush pomegranate, cumin and onion seeds with a rolling pin.
3. Mix all ingredients except butter; knead to a soft dough with water.
4. Shape into balls and roll out into 6"-diameter pancakes.
5. Cook on a griddle (*tawa*) or in a tandoor until brown on both sides.
6. Remove from fire, apply butter and serve hot.

KHASTA ROTI

(Wholewheat oven-baked bread)

Serves: 4-5   Preparation time: 25 minutes   Cooking time: 10-15 minutes

Ingredients

Wholewheat flour (*atta*) *500 gm / 2 ½ cups*
Salt to taste, Sugar *12 gm / 2 ½ tsp*
Carom (*ajwain*) seeds *15 gm / 1 tbsp*
Water *300 ml / 1 ½ cups*

Method

1. Sieve flour; add salt, sugar and carom seeds. Knead into a hard dough with water. Cover with a moist cloth and keep aside for 15 minutes.
2. Divide the dough into 10 balls. Dust and roll into 10 cm *rotis*. Prick with a fork evenly.
3. Bake the *rotis* in an oven at 175 °C / 350 °F for 8-10 minutes or till light brown in colour.

GLOSSARY OF COOKING TERMS

Bake : Cook in an oven or on a hot surface without direct exposure to a flame.

Baste : Moisten meat, poultry or game during roasting by spooning over it, its juices.

Batter : A mixture of flour, egg and milk / water used in cooking.

Blanch : Immerse in boiling water so that the peel comes off.

Croquettes : Fried mixtures of meat, fish, poultry or potatoes bound into various shapes.

Devein : Remove the main central vein from a fish.

Fillet : The undercut of a loin or ribs of meat, boned sides of fish or boned breasts of poultry.

Grill : Cook on a grill (device on a cooker for radiating heat downwards).

Marinade : A seasoned mixture of oil, vinegar, lemon juice, etc. in which meat, poultry and fish is left for some time to soften its fibres and add flavour to it.

Roast : Cook in an oven or in open heat.

Sauté : Fry quickly over strong heat in fat or oil.

Simmer : Keep boiling gently on low heat.

Skewer : Fasten together pieces of food compactly on a specially designed long pin, for cooking.

Whisk : To beat air rapidly into a mixture with an egg beater, rotary beater or electric beater.

INDEX

NON-VEGETARIAN

VEGETARIAN

94

ACCOMPANIMENTS

ACKNOWLEDGEMENTS

Grateful thanks to the Master Chefs at **The Intercontinental Hotel,** New Delhi, and the **Oberoi Group of Hotels,** New Delhi, for making available their kitchens for the preparation and photography of the dishes.

ISBN: 1-85605-581-7

Published in 2000 by **Silverdale Books**
An imprint of **Bookmart Ltd**
Registered Number 2372865
Trading as Bookmart Limited
Desford Road, Enderby
Leicester, LE9 5AD

© **Roli Books Pvt. Ltd. 1999**
Tel.: 91 (011) 6442271, 6462782, Fax: 91 (011) 6467185
E-mail: roli@vsnl.com, Website: rolibooks.com

Photographs: Dheeraj Paul

Printed in Singapore